PEGASUS
Library

Werner Schmalenbach

Henri Rousseau

Dreams
of the Jungle

Prestel

Munich · London · New York

Front cover: *The Hungry Lion*, 1905, detail
(see pp. 28–29)
Spine: *Exotic Landscape*, 1910, detail
(see pp. 52–53)
Frontispiece: *Scout Attacked by a Tiger*, 1904, detail
(see p. 21)

Translated from the German by Jenny Marsh
Copyedited by Kirk Marlow

Library of Congress Card Number: 00-102986

© Prestel Verlag, Munich · London· New York, 2000

Prestel Verlag
Mandlstrasse 26 · 80802 Munich
Tel. (089) 38 17 09-0, Fax (089) 38 17 09-35
e-mail: sales@prestel.de;
4 Bloomsbury Place · London WCiA 2QA
Tel. (020) 7323 5004, Fax (020) 7636 8004
e-mail: sales@prestel-uk.co.uk;
175 Fifth Avenue, Suite 402, New York, NY 10010
Tel. (212) 995 27 20, Fax (212) 995 2733
e-mail: sales@prestel-usa.com

Designed by WIGEL, Munich
Paperback cover designed by Matthias Hauer, Munich
Lithography by ReproLine, Munich
Printed and bound by Passavia Druckservice, Passau

Printed in Germany on acid-free paper

ISBN 3-7913-2409-8 (paperback)
ISBN 3-7913-1942-6 (hardback)

Contents

The "Customs Officer" in his Beloved Paris

A small life. But a great artist. How can, or how should we understand this? It remains a puzzle. Of course, the emergence of a great artist is always a puzzle. It is never explicable, either through the living conditions of the artist, or through those of society, or of the times. It always remains the great, incomprehensible exception, even when — not the case with Henri Rousseau — it merges organically into the general trend of art history. It is all the more puzzling when a great artist never, ever, to the end of his life, steps outside the narrow sphere from which he comes.

Throughout his life Rousseau remained the petit bourgeois in the same humble conditions from which he came. He was born in 1844 in the French town of Laval, the son of a tinsmith. Like every other young man then, he completed his schooling and did military service. Nothing remarkable happened during this time. He was never, as legend has it, and as was believed for a long time and as he himself on occasion stated, a soldier in Mexico, nor did he — this again a firmly upheld legend that pleased him — help to protect the population of the northern French town of Dreux in 1870 from the horrors of the Franco-Prussian war. His was a life devoid of glamor and devoid of exciting incidents.

In 1872, at the age of twenty-eight, he entered the service of the *Octroi*, the Parisian customs service, which he left only in 1893 after more than twenty years. He took up residence in Montparnasse in the petit bourgeois quarter that delighted in the name of Plaisance and, despite frequent moves,

Henri Rousseau
Photograph, 1895

Left:
Toll Station
ca. 1890
Oil on canvas
14 ¾ × 12 ⅞ in.
(37.5 × 32.5 cm)
London, Courtauld
Institute Galleries

never left it. There he mixed with the ordinary people of the *quartier*, especially when after leaving the customs service he got into financial difficulties and gave music and art lessons in the neighborhood. Even when, in his last years, artists and intellectuals from a new, much younger generation entered his life, nothing changed in his general disposition or in his simple way of life. The horizon of his feelings and thoughts remained the same, even when he finally discovered the jungle as his great artistic theme. In his painting he dreamed of far-off, exotic worlds, but he himself, the dreamer, remained firmly within the narrow confines of his *quartier*, unlike his sometime neighbor, Paul Gauguin, only a few years younger than himself.

Thus it came about that he was known as *le douanier* (the customs officer), long after he left the customs service, indeed, long after his death. The French have a special name for the officials who monitor incoming and outgoing goods and levy tolls at the city gates and at the quaysides along the river. According to this, Rousseau was a *gabelou*. Nevertheless, it became customary to call him "*Le Douanier*." The conditions in which he performed his duties at the old fortifications of Paris are illustrated beautifully in his painting *Toll Station* (illus. p. 6). As we see, here the city is still green. A barred gateway stands half-open. A toll collector guards the entrance, and another stands high up above him on a wall. Rousseau could have been either one of these officers.

Customs officers on duty at Saint Nicolas Harbor, in front of the Pont du Carrousel. Photo: Bibliothèque historique de la Ville de Paris

Right:
Myself,
Portrait-Landscape
1890
Oil on canvas
56 $\frac{1}{4}$ × 43 $\frac{1}{4}$ in.
(143 × 110 cm)
Prague, National Gallery

He belonged to Paris. Even though he was born and raised elsewhere, he was nevertheless a part of it. Paris was his city. He portrayed it incessantly, not as a great, splendid metropolis, but rather in its modest, "small-town" aspects. As a painter he took no notice of the "Grands

Boulevards" created during his lifetime under the aegis of Baron Georges-Eugène Haussmann at the expense of large areas of old Paris; in this, he differed from his contemporaries, the Impressionists, who found their favorite motifs precisely here — in "big-city" Paris. But, again contrary to them, Rousseau was full of enthusiasm for the Eiffel Tower, erected for the World Exposition of 1889. It was not only the painters of the Académie, headed by the respected Salon painter Adolphe William Bouguereau — who was among the signatories to a petition to prevent the construction of the epoch-making edifice — who were passionately opposed to the "monster." The Impressionists, too — in other words, the avant-garde among contemporary painters who had nothing in common with an artist such as Bouguereau — were vehemently against the building of the Eiffel Tower. Rousseau had none of these prejudices. The bold iron structure soaring up into the sky filled him with such joy that he memorialized it in his large, full-length self-portrait of 1890 (illus. p. 9), which he painted under the influence of the World Exposition. It was his innocent optimism that made him include in his painting the tower and an iron bridge — completely unacceptable in artistic terms of that time — over the Seine, as well as the captive hot-air balloon that floated above the city for the duration of the exhibition: as participants in the great spectacle that delighted him, but also as harbingers of a new age, which he nevertheless thereafter only rarely and incidentally glorified in his art. In the end, in his last years, the animals of the jungle became more important to him than the Eiffel Tower. Still, this was an astonishing mix that he himself, free from any sort of ideology, probably hardly noticed as such, especially since he even found the most important of his sources of inspiration for his jungles in that very city of Paris — namely,

Edouard Manet
The World Exposition, 1867
1867
Oil on canvas
42 ½ × 77 ⅜ in.
(108 × 196.5 cm)
Oslo, Nasjonalgalleriet

in the Jardin des Plantes, the botanical garden, to which he made repeated pilgrimages in order to study the tropical plants and exotic animals. He once told the art critic Arsène Alexandre: "When I step into the hothouses and see the plants from exotic lands, it seems to me that I am in a dream."

Included in the great spectacle of the World Exhibition that fascinated Parisians for half a year, and that aroused in them patriotic feelings that were all the more pronounced since the event coincided with the centenary of the French Revolution, were the pavilions of distant regions of the world, above all, of course, those from the French colonies: villages from Tonkin, Senegal, and Indochina were erected there, as well as a "Mexican palace" with plants and animals from the tropics. This was a triumph of colonialism, utterly undimmed by any conflicts of conscience. In his vaudeville in three acts entitled *Une Visite à l'Exhibition de 1889*, Rousseau waxed enthusiastic about "this great exhibition, where there is the Eiffel Tower, the Trocadero, negroes, redskins." Two years later he painted his first jungle picture, which would be followed, after an interval of more than ten years, from 1905 onwards, by all the others, during the last six years of his life.

According to Rousseau's own repeated testimony, he started to paint when he was forty, in other words, in the mid-1880s. A little later, in 1890, while still working for the municipal customs service, he created his large-format self-portrait with the proud title *Myself* and the additional words *Portrait-Landscape* to describe the genre, which he believed was his own invention (illus. p. 9). Here he saw himself as the total artist, a giant before the backdrop of the city, towering above everything else: the tiny people along the bank of the Seine, the trees, the houses, the boat with its bright flags and the Eiffel Tower. Still, however high he reaches into the sky and however self-confidently he bears the insignia of his handiwork — beret on head, brush in one hand and palette in the other — it cannot be disguised that even here he is the "little man" who is totally unaware that he is the great artist as whom he is posing. His demonstrative pride as an artist cannot hide the modesty of his artistic existence.

Painters of the Académie

Rousseau occasionally called himself a great painter. But he cannot have felt that he actually was one. Otherwise, he would not have nurtured throughout his life the impossible dream of being acknowledged as a painter of the Académie des Beaux-Arts. All his life he harbored an ambivalence between healthy self-confidence and feelings of inferiority. Certainly, he had the highest admiration for the work of Eugène Delacroix. Yet he also admired painters of high repute in his day whose names have long since been wiped from our memory and whose works have vanished into the basements of French museums. Who still knows their names now — the history painters

William Adolphe
Bouguereau
The Rape of Psyche
1895
Private collection

of those days, the painters of battles, the genre painters, the Salon painters, the Orientalists? Who still recognizes the name of even a once-celebrated painter such as Jean-Léon Gérôme? Rousseau often said that he had a lot to thank him for; it could even be that *The Two Majesties* (illus. p. 13), one of Gérôme's paintings depicting a lion on a rocky shore gazing at the sun as it sets over the sea, inspired one of Rousseau's most beautiful paintings, *The Sleeping Gypsy* (illus. p. 26). Rousseau regularly visited the "official" Salon of the Société des Artistes Français, to which he had no chance of ever being admitted and which was regarded with horror by the modern artists of his time. On the death of Bouguereau in 1905, whose paintings were the epitome of Salon kitsch of the second half of the nineteenth century, Rousseau was filled with "une emotion profonde," (deep emotion). At the same time, however, he admired the great masters of the past. In 1884 the Ministry of Culture granted him a copyist's permit, which gave him free entrance to the national museums — the Louvre, the Palais Luxembourg, and the châteaux of Versailles and Saint-Germain. He made liberal use of it, but we know little about his special preferences.

Rousseau may have held the virtuoso skills of academic painters up before his eyes as a distant goal. If this was the case, then it was fortunate that he was never able to achieve this goal; his artistic genius was stronger than his ideals and his idols. It is true that he, like they, permitted himself no liberties as a painter, but the demand for completeness which he set for each of his paintings was something quite different from that of the academic painters. Since for him a picture could not be considered complete until each and every tiny section had been painted over, he was still able to say in 1907, looking at works by Cézanne: "You know, I could finish all these paintings."

No traces of his admiration for the "official" art of his time can be found in his work. Perhaps he admired — and envied — these painters for their great fame rather than their painting. Certainly it was the case that he, self-taught, marveled at the phenomenal naturalistic handiwork of such painters without recognizing that he himself belonged to a generation of artists who, in historical terms, had dealt a death blow to the perfected naturalism of all this "official" art. With his year of birth, 1844, Rousseau fell exactly halfway between Claude Monet, born in 1840, and Gauguin, born in 1848, and thus between the generations of the Impressionists and the Post-Impressionists, closer artistically to the latter undoubtedly than to the former. And yet his birth date hardly defines his position in history.

Jean-Léon Gérôme
(1824–1904)
The Two Majesties
1883
Oil on canvas,
27 ⅛ × 50 ⅞ in.
(69 × 129 cm)
Private collection

The reason that it is hardly possible to define Rousseau's position in the art of the end of the nineteenth century and beginning of the twentieth is that he did not participate in the formulation of questions and in the innovations of the age. Or might we be mistaken? Should we not consider Rousseau just as much an important individual artistic figure as the other great painters of the turn of the century — such as Paul Gauguin, Georges Seurat, Vincent van Gogh, Henri de Toulouse-Lautrec, and Edvard Munch, all of whom, like him, were misunderstood and treated with hostility? We are reluctant to place him in these ranks, since he was not just different, but different in a way unlike the others. After all, they were not all eccentrics, while Rousseau was. They were all far from being considered naive. They had all been taught to paint, they had had teachers and studied art, even if they quickly discarded what they had learned. They appeared to be supremely confident about their art, and they did not suffer from inferiority complexes vis-à-vis the efforts of successful contemporary artists. In none of them was there this great, fundamental self-deception that we see in Rousseau, this gap between the putative artistic ideal and actual genius. None of them would have been able to present themselves as artists in such an innocent and yet self-confident manner as did Rousseau in his self-portrait of 1890. There is no comparability, even if, viewed from an art-historical perspective, there is much that links him with Gauguin as well as with Seurat and other painters of that generation. He remains, to a greater degree than the others, a unique case in art history. Rousseau was great as the self-taught painter that he was. And thus it is touching that, in a self-portrayal in 1907, he wrote: "If my parents had known of my gift for painting, like our dead Clément himself told them...then today I would be the greatest and wealthiest painter in France."

Trees, Forests

The central theme of Rousseau's painting was from beginning to end — in other words, even in the years when jungles became the dominant motif in his work — the streets of Paris, the bridges over the Seine, the quaysides along the river, the level crossings, and the parks. Sometimes the subjects were also villages in the regions around Paris, on the Marne, on the Oise, and now and then the countryside, with trees, cows, and haystacks. But Paris was primarily his theme. He frequently used picture postcards as his models. Looking at his paintings one realizes how green Paris was in those days. Hardly ever are his townscapes totally devoid of trees: he must have loved trees above everything else. Given his tendency towards extremely objective, linear precision, it is remarkable that he showed such devotion to the themes of tree and forest — and finally jungle — since by their very nature, these are subjects that one rather expects to receive summary treatment. For Rousseau every single leaf counted, at least those in the foreground of his pictures. In the Jardin des Plantes, which he visited so often and with such pleasure, he studied trees and leaves in even the tiniest detail, as we can see from surviving pencil drawings. He did however sketch trees "in the flesh," so to speak, with a freedom that he never permitted himself in his finished pictures. What he noted down summarily in his sketches — often of great aesthetic appeal — was translated in the paintings into a neat agglomeration of branches, twigs, and leaves. There are about ten surviving examples in his artistic oeuvre that demonstrate this step from the free sketch to the definitive work. It is as though the artist was neglecting to use a proficiency that was

Drawing
Oak Twig

Study for Family Fishing
ca. 1895
Oil on canvas
7 ½ × 11 ⅞ in.
(19 × 29 cm)
New York, Sam Spiegel
Collection

Family Fishing
ca. 1895
Oil on canvas
14 ¾ × 18 in.
(37.5 × 45.7 cm)
Private collection

obviously within his grasp. These sketches are often called "impressionistic." This is erroneous, as Impressionism cannot be defined merely through loose brushwork. Rousseau was never affected by Impressionism, he never employed the "comma script" of the Impressionists, he never made us of the prismatic breakdown of color, and he never regarded as his concern the liberation of color from the object and as an end in itself. His sketches had a tonal quality — in other words, they were pre-Impressionist in character and their freedom was just that of the brushstroke and was restricted to the

sketches. Whereas the paintings have the character of a drawing — in Heinrich Wölfflin's terminology — the sketches give a "painterly" effect: fleeting impressions which as such have nothing to do with Impressionism. They were simply sketches, devoid of any stylistic intent, provisional jottings that he typically did not sign. Despite their provisional character, however, they often have a great, very artistic density. Rousseau himself regarded them as unfinished, and therefore incomplete and imperfect. He obviously had at his command an artistic freedom which he, however, did not "need" for his art: he was concerned with other things — works that have the character of finality and permanence. It is strange that Rousseau's later admirer, the young American painter Max Weber, who often visited him and bought works from him, preferred the sketches to the finished versions, a preference with which he did not do justice to his artist friend.

In 1886 Rousseau exhibited a lovely painting entitled *A Carnival Evening* (illus. p. 17) in the Salon des Indépendants. There has been astonishment that the artist, who after all dated the beginning of his painting career only to the mid-1880s, should have set out on his artistic path with a masterpiece of such maturity, however little his contemporaries may have recognized this. How was it possible that a master just 'fell from the sky' like this? He must surely have tried his hand at painting earlier, although we have no evidence for this. If there were earlier attempts, they have remained in obscurity.

Walking in the Forest
ca. 1886
Oil on canvas
27 ½ × 23 ⅞ in.
(70 × 60.5 cm)
Zurich, Kunsthaus
Zurich

Rendezvous in the Forest
1889
Oil on canvas
36 ¼ × 28 ¾ in.
(92 × 73 cm)
Washington, D.C.,
National Gallery of Art

A Carnival Evening
1886
Oil on canvas
42 ⅛ × 35 ⅛ in.
(106.9 × 89.3 cm)
Philadelphia Museum
of Art, Louis E. Stern
Collection

    A Carnival Evening already shows the basic compositional scheme of most of his jungle paintings, which would follow ten years later: an incident involving two protagonists in the center foreground, in front of a high backdrop of trees under the white full moon, which is usually replaced by the sun in the jungle paintings. What in the latter generally becomes a duel between wild animals or between man and beast is here a pair of lovers dressed up as Harlequin and Pierrette. The moonlight casts its spell over everything: the two costumed figures in the wintry night, the bare trees with their twigs and branches of utmost delicacy, and the clouds in the sky.

Closely related to this are two other paintings that must have been produced in the next few years: *Rendezvous in the Forest*, in which a kissing couple in fancy dress traverses a forest on horseback, and *Walking in the Forest* (both illus. p. 16), in which a woman dressed in city clothing, a furled umbrella in her right hand, pauses during her walk through the trees, alerted by something — a noise, perhaps — which causes her to put her left hand over her heart as she looks back.

The Salon des Indépendents

With *A Carnival Evening* Rousseau made his first appearance at the Salon des Indépendants, which would become an important forum for him. With very few interruptions, he exhibited there each year until his death in 1910. It appears that Paul Signac, who had been among the founders of the Salon the previous year, encouraged him to take part. The Salon was "independent" to the degree that participation was not subject to any jury (unlike the conservative Salon des Artistes Français, known simply as "the Salon"); anybody who wished to could take part. This was its great weakness, but also its strength, since it offered a platform for many young painters who were not welcome in the "official" Salon. Here one could see works by such painters as Seurat, Toulouse-Lautrec, van Gogh, and later Pierre Bonnard, Henri Matisse, and many others, and here Rousseau became acquainted with their work and doubtless also with the painters themselves. We do not know what effect this had on him; it was probably not of great significance for his own creative work.

If the Salon des Indépendants offered a chance to many untalented painters, including many "Sunday painters," it also presented an opportunity — initially the only one — for Rousseau, who exposed himself there to the ridicule of visitors and critics for years on end, as did for a time the other great painters of the *fin de siècle*; they too were controversial. To that extent Rousseau was not a special case. In 1889, one critic wrote that he had never seen anything more grotesque than Rousseau's portraits and van Gogh's *Starry Night*, thus lumping these two painters together. It is not known how much Rousseau suffered from the constant mockery he endured there for many years. Strangely he kept all these reviews — almost all negative — pasted into a notebook. Nevertheless, the Salon des Indépendants became a sort of home for him. Here in 1890 he showed his large self-portrait. Years later he paid homage to the Salon with the richly figural allegorical painting entitled *Liberty Inviting Artists to Take Part in the Twenty-second Exhibition of the Société des Artistes Indépendants* (illus. p. 64). In 1910 Signac, as a representative of the Salon, was among the few who attended Rousseau's funeral.

1891: The First Jungle Painting

Rousseau showed his first jungle painting in the Salon des Indépendants —
the seventh such event — in the year following his self-portrait. Only years
later would this be followed by his second jungle painting, and then all the
others on that theme. The title is *Surprise!*: in a storm-lashed jungle, under
a rainy sky lit up by flashes of lightning, a tiger comes across something
that surprises it, or that is surprised by it; both the title and the painting itself
leave this open to conjecture. Snarling, with fangs bared, the magnificent
tiger creeps up on its prey, which is hidden from the viewer's gaze. The strong
movement of the forest, which, however, barely affects the plants in the foreground, differentiates the painting from Rousseau's later ones of the jungle,
which are all totally motionless. Only on a single other occasion did he paint

Surprise!
1891
Oil on canvas
51 ¼ × 63 ⅞ in.
(130 × 162 cm)
London, The Trustees
of the National Gallery

a scene with similarly wild movement, and that was of a cruiser in a thunderstorm on tumultuous seas (1890–1893; Paris, Musée de l'Orangerie, Jean Walter – Paul Guillaume Collection).

Despite the strong sense of movement, *Surprise!* has the character of a formal, completely balanced tapestry, rich and harmonious in its color tones. The plants — indeed, the individual leaves — are painted piece by piece, each clearly separated, in their formal composition untouched by wind and weather. The extraordinary thing is the extravagant wealth of the color gradations within a large unit of color, particularly the rich variations in the greens and the occasional gleam of red leaves, but also the true ingenuity of the dark plants in the right foreground and the dark tree trunks behind. The painting is dominated by abundance — even superabundance — and unity at one and the same time. Such a skillful picture can only be composed by a master, and the designation of "naive painting" seems less convincing.

Even at that time people were reminded of the pictorial woven hangings of the fifteenth century with their rich floral motifs, for example, tapestries such as *La Dame à la licorne* (*The Lady with the Unicorn*), which was discovered in the 1840s and later acquired by the Musée de Cluny, where Rousseau frequently saw it. It is entirely possible that this was one of his sources of inspiration. Given his pronounced sense for the fantastic, his sense also for the proliferation of rich vegetation, and not least his sense for the decorative, these pictorial weavings must have inspired him. The manner in which, in *Surprise!*, he portrays the forest, arranges the plants in the foreground into flat strips, and avoids empty space, is all in fact reminiscent of the pictorial weavings of the late Middle Ages.

"La Dame à la licorne,"
Tapestry, 15th century
(detail)
Paris, Musée de Cluny

But there were also other sources of inspiration, and the tiger points to one. The way in which the animal is set in the painting, and how it barely bends a stem as it creeps up on its prey, makes it seem like an extraneous insertion, even if it has been incorporated into the whole. As in so many other cases, Rousseau painted the tiger from a model — in this case, from a pastel drawing by Delacroix (illus. p. 22), whose important exhibition he had seen at the Ecole des Beaux-Arts in 1885 and for whom he had a particular admiration. The same tiger reappeared much later in *Scout Attacked by a Tiger*, this time moving from right to left. However, it is not the fact that Rousseau based his tiger on a model, but rather what he did with it that is of significance. Many great painters, up to Picasso and beyond, quoted works by earlier artists, and not a few — including, on many occasions, Rousseau — based their work on photographs. Rousseau's tiger has little more in common with Delacroix's tiger than the position of its body. The verve with which the model was drawn was not important for Rousseau, nor was he interested in the "picturesque" aspect. He was concerned solely with the bodily posture of the beast of prey and, stylistically, with its incorporation into its surroundings, with its harmonization with the rhythm of the picture, which is quite different from that into which Delacroix's tiger fits. Rousseau did not "stylize" his model; he simplified it and interpreted it in color.

Rousseau's preoccupation with Delacroix on one occasion showed itself in a direct copy of *Encounter of a Lion and a Tiger*, where he keeps surprisingly close to the treatment of the original painting, denying his own linear, totally unpainterly style to such an extent that one has to ask oneself why Delacroix in particular fascinated him so much. The answer must lie in the motif: in Delacroix's suggestive depiction of exotic wild beasts in combat. Nevertheless, the copy shows that Rousseau had the definite ability to paint as freely, in as "painterly" a manner, as his revered predecessor, but he made no use of this ability in his art. This is strikingly manifested in *Surprise!*; with the boldness of his great success, with the naturalness and self-confidence of his painting, and with a totally different quality from the work of Delacroix despite all his admiration for him, Rousseau gives notice of his own idiom. He must have been aware of this, but he never commented on it. He followed his own path, alone, unflustered and unwavering.

Eugène Delacroix
*Encounter of a Lion
and a Tiger*
1828–29
9 ½ x 12 ½ in.
(24 × 32 cm)
Prague, National Gallery

Henri Rousseau
Tiger Attacking a Lion
Copy after Delacroix
1885
Prague, National Gallery

A young painter from French-speaking Switzerland, Félix Vallotton, then still unknown, who shortly afterwards became a member of the Nabis group together with Pierre Bonnard, Edouard Vuillard, and others, wrote the following lines about Rousseau's *Surprise!* in an article in the *Gazette de Lausanne* concerning the seventh Salon des Indépendants in 1891:

"Monsieur Rousseau amazes us year after year. He forces himself upon us and every time succeeds in getting himself noticed. Backs [of people] jostle in front of his entries, and the place rocks with laughter. He is a dreadful neighbor, he overpowers everything else. We see a tiger surprising its prey. This is the alpha and omega of painting, so bewildering that deeply rooted convictions falter and waver before so much self-satisfaction and such great childlikeness. Everybody stops laughing. It is always wonderful to observe a conviction, of whatever sort, given such relentless expression. For my part, I sincerely appreciate these efforts, and I prefer them a hundred times to the regrettable mistakes all around."

The "alpha and omega of painting": nobody else was writing about Rousseau at that time in the same sort of terms as Vallotton, but the friendly voices multiplied. Quite a few comments made by artists of repute have come down to us, although their authenticity is uncertain. Thus, Camille Pissarro is said to have spoken about the "naivety of the drawing, the quality of this art, the rightness of the values and the richness of the tones" when faced with Rousseau's paintings in the Salon des Indépendants, among them *A Carnival Evening*. His Impressionist colleague Renoir is reported by the art dealer Ambroise Vollard to have said of a picture by Rousseau: "What a beautiful color tone....I am certain Ingres would not have disdained this." At the sight of Rousseau's self-portrait, Gauguin is supposed to have exclaimed: "There is the truth and the future! There is painting!" And Odilon Redon, the Symbolist painter, is said in 1888 to have praised the "genius of this painter...that sometimes elevates itself to classical beauty."

It seems, however, that the very first encouragement came from a completely unexpected source, namely from such academic painters as Jean-Léon Gérôme, and Félix Clément, the one-time director of the Société des Beaux-Arts in Lyons, who was from Rousseau's home town of Laval. On occasion Rousseau stated that he would always owe him a debt of gratitude since he always gave him good advice. Towards the end of his life he also told a critic: "If I have kept my naivety, it is because Monsieur Gérôme always told me I should keep it." This was an astonishing revelation, making it seem as though Rousseau had had a choice, which in truth he did not have. In brief biographical notes dating from 1895 he speaks of the many disappointments that he experienced "alone, with no teacher but nature and with some advice from Gérôme and Clément." In the same context he calls himself a realistic painter. All of these are strange contradictions, which are continually cropping up in connection with Rousseau.

1893: War

War
1894
Oil on canvas
44 ⁷⁄₈ × 76 ⁷⁄₈ in.
(114 × 195 cm)
Paris, Musée d'Orsay,
Galerie du Jeu de
Paume

More than ten years passed before Rousseau was again gripped by the theme of the jungle, never to relinquish it. During these interim years he developed, through a whole series of works, into something far beyond a mere painter of Parisian cityscapes, although he continued to paint these as well until the end of his life.

In 1893 he created an extraordinary painting, *War*, almost two meters in width. A woman with long black hair, wearing a bizarre, frayed white

dress and holding a torch in one hand and a sword in the other, is galloping across a wide landscape on the back of a nag whose red tongue dangles from its muzzle. Below the horse's hooves lie the pale corpses of the dead and dying. Black ravens perch on them, bloody scraps of flesh in their beaks. This is an apocalyptic allegory of War — in every respect a singular work within Rousseau's oeuvre. The picture was hung in the Salon des Indépendants in 1894 and impressed the very young, still unknown poet Alfred Jarry, whose well-known play *Ubu Roi* was written a few years later. (In the 1920s this play would assume a central position in Surrealist thinking.) Jarry, who came from Rousseau's hometown, made the acquaintance of the painter and sometimes lodged in his house when he was in financial difficulties. Rousseau executed a portrait of Jarry, now vanished. For *L'Ymagier*, a quarterly journal published by Jarry and Rémy de Gourmont, the spokesman of the Paris Symbolists, in which primarily folk art — *imagerie populaire* — appeared alongside prints of Old Masters, the publishers reproduced a lithograph that Rousseau had made for this purpose from *War*. Jarry was the first of the intellectuals to defend the *Douanier's* painting, more than a decade before Guillaume Apollinaire, who became Rousseau's most important advocate in his last few years.

Rousseau's contemporaries were particularly struck by the deep black of the horse, the birds, the tree on the left, and the large leaves on the tree on the right-hand side of *War*. Gauguin is said to have expressed his complete admiration of Rousseau's black. In fact the effect was bold, since the Impressionists, who wanted everything to be light and colorful, had banned black from the palette as a "non-color." Black dominates in a whole series of prominent paintings by Rousseau: in *Myself, Portrait-Landscape* of 1890, the *Portrait of Pierre Loti* of about 1891 (illus. pp. 9, 27), and his full-length portraits of women (illus. p. 78). Probably without himself being aware of it, Rousseau had breached some barrier with his use of black.

1897: The Sleeping Gypsy

Many other works were created during these years: *A Centenary of Independence* (illus. p. 63), *Artillery Men* (illus. p. 74), two large full-length portraits of women (one of which was much later acquired by Picasso), *The Merry Jesters* (illus. p. 51), *Child with Doll* (illus. p. 79), *The Wedding* (illus. p. 76), and a self-portrait with a portrait of his second wife as a pendant (both Paris, Musée du Louvre; Dotation Picasso) — a diptych, so to speak. There were many other paintings of larger or smaller format, and always the views of Paris.

Most importantly, however, in 1897 he created one of his principal works, *The Sleeping Gypsy*, its format of 1.3 × 5 meters making it one of his largest and most unusual paintings. Rousseau himself wrote a description on the picture frame: "The cat, although wild, hesitates to pounce on its prey who is fast asleep from exhaustion." In the futile hope of selling this painting to his home town of Laval, he wrote the mayor a letter in which he gave the following description:

The Sleeping Gypsy
1897
Oil on canvas
51 x 79 in.
(129.5 × 500.7 cm)
New York, The
Museum of Modern Art

"A wandering negress, a mandolin player, sleeps in deep exhaustion, her jug beside her [a pitcher of drinking water]. A lion happens to pass that way and sniffs at her but does not devour her. The scene takes place in a completely dry desert. The gypsy is dressed in oriental fashion."

Portrait of Pierre Loti
ca. 1891
Oil on canvas
24 × 19 ¾ in.
(61 × 50 cm)
Zurich, Kunsthaus
Zurich

This wonderful painting is so very different from all of Rousseau's other works that it was often suspected of being a forgery, until the letter to the mayor of Laval became known. None of Rousseau's other works is set in a totally treeless waste. Nowhere else is the confrontation between human and animal so peaceful. No other painting by the artist possesses a comparable monumentality, and nowhere are human figure and "beast" portrayed as large as here. The painting is dominated by the infinite stillness of a night with a full moon during which a placid lion happens upon an exotic dark-haired woman asleep, wrapped in a brightly colored striped robe. Dumb witnesses to the encounter are her walking stick, the mandolin, and the water jug. The setting is a barren waste in a hilly desert crossed — strangely enough — by an expanse of water. This is a fantastic vision, born from the painter's imagination, for which one can find no model in art. The work is unique within the artist's oeuvre, unlike his jungle scenes, which so often involve variations on a basic theme. It is also unique in the history of painting.

Nevertheless, the painting could be seen in connection with Orientalism, which was in vogue around that time and was actually rather more than a mere fashion, since even such great painters as Delacroix and Jean-Auguste-Dominique Ingres took their material from North Africa and the Near East. People gazed, full of fascination, at depictions of such countries as Algeria, Morocco, Egypt, Palestine, and Arabia, with their overwhelming color, their profligate splendor, their harems and palaces, their religious pomp, both Islamic and biblical, their wild battles and erotic excesses, their blandishments and their dark perils: everything that contemporary revues and travel reports put before their eyes in pictures and words.

Rousseau did not follow up these enticements. Gérôme, whom he considered a kind of mentor, was elected as honorary president of the Société des Artistes Orientalistes towards the end of the century, when Orientalism had long since run its course. But Rousseau was no Orientalist. The Orient did not concern him. He was enchanted by the jungle and wild animals, subject matter beyond the bounds of history.

Nevertheless, he did create a portrait — an idealized portrait — of the novelist Pierre Loti, much read at that time, who had traveled widely in the Near and Far East, although Rousseau portrayed him in anything but an Oriental setting. There are even four ordinary factory chimneys rising in the distance. Only the fez that Loti wears on his head is a reminder of the East. And, instead of the opulent colors of the Orient, here again it is deepest black that dominates.

The Hungry Lion
1905
Oil on canvas
83 x 122 in.
(210.5 x 310.5 cm)
Basel, Ernst Beyeler
Collection

1905–1910: The Jungle Paintings

The first jungle painting — *Surprise!* — with a tiger stalking its unseen prey, was created in 1891 (illus. p. 19). Despite all the uncertainty about the dating of his works, Rousseau's series of jungle scenes must have resumed again in 1905. That was the year in which he showed a massive painting at the Salon d'Automne (the Parisian Autumn Salon), over three meters in width, entitled *The Hungry Lion* (illus. pp. 28–29). The painting presents the basic scheme of Rousseau's jungle pictures: in the center foreground the scene of combat, surrounded by gigantic plants that partially shield the background and the sky in the middle ground and in the upper sections. The scene in the foreground is of a lion attacking an antelope, its teeth and claws ripping deep into the body. The next level is filled with trees with dark trunks, branches and twigs and large leaves of various shapes. Other wild creatures lurk in the dense foliage: a spotted panther waiting for its share of the prey, and two birds holding bloody strips of flesh torn from the dying antelope, while on the left of the picture we sense the presence of a large dark animal, perhaps a gorilla. Towards the top of the painting the foliage thins out and allows glimpses of a cloud shaped like a mountain, as well as the red setting sun.

Again everything is arranged parallel to the picture plane, with few spatial references, again comparable to tapestries of the late Middle Ages or — as was often remarked on at the time — Persian miniatures. This is a large, splendid symphony in green, made up of innumerable hues which give the picture its extraordinary richness and sensory density. The viewer's gaze feasts on the profusion of colors. Botanists have been able to identify most of the plants and trees, but this is of no importance to the artistic eye. The great number of shades of green has also been counted, but that too is

An illustration from ca. 1842 from *Musée des Familles*

insignificant, because of course it is not the number but the profusion of greens that impresses the eye, together with the overwhelming richness and extreme simplicity.

Unlike *Surprise!* complete stillness reigns in *The Hungry Lion*. Not a single leaf moves. Even the lion's deadly attack on its victim takes place without the slightest action, devoid of anything dramatic. One senses that Rousseau also painted this scene after a model, possibly from the depiction of a black panther devouring an antelope that he could have found in *Musée des Familles*, a popular publication of 1842 (illus. p. 30). Here he sets his protagonists in the painting but barely integrates them into it, as though they were props from a totally different play. What is happening in the foreground has little to do with the general scene. As on a stage, it takes place against the massive backdrop of the forest. Everything is painted in a manner totally devoid of mystery. Rousseau employs no "symbolistic" tools of any kind to suggest the *mystère* upon which Gauguin focused in his paintings done in Brittany and later in many of his works done in the South Seas. Despite all the fantasy, Rousseau's painting remains objective. He paints what he has seen and studied in the Jardin des Plantes and in illustrated publications, transposing it into a dreamed-up, and yet dreamless, primeval forest. He paints without emotion, but the effect of *The Hungry Lion* — like that of all his paintings — is emotional. One clearly senses that he has never in his life seen the actual jungle. The forest is domesticated, and one does not credit the wild beasts with savagery, not even when they administer the *coup de grace*. Exaggerating a little, one could say that this is a forest consisting of houseplants, cultivated plants from a greenhouse, and trees from a garden — in other words, a jungle on the scale of a botanical garden, of Rousseau's beloved Jardin des Plantes.

The Salon d'Automne, where Rousseau showed this painting (which the public could hardly ignore in view of its huge dimensions) in 1905, had been founded two years earlier. But it was only in 1905 that the Salon became important for art history as it proved to be the stage for the first, spectacular appearance of a group of young artists to whom was given the name of les Fauves, the "wild beasts" — initially, as so often in art history, with an ironic intention. These painters advocated and practiced an art of color that was "wild," expressive, if almost always held in check by the great authority of Cézanne. Their art, which today appears moderate, was then revolutionary and directly preceded the Cubist revolution by only a few years. If the Cubists advocated the liberation of form from objects, the Fauves liberated color. The oldest of the group was Matisse, to whom younger artists rallied, including André Derain, Maurice Vlaminck, Raoul Dufy, Albert Marquet, Othon Friesz, and several others. Goerges Rouault was also once counted among their number. Paintings by these rebellious artists were hung in the central room of the Salon d'Automne, which a critic called the *cage aux fauves* (the "wild beasts' cage"), and right in the midst of them was Rousseau's

LE SALON D'AUTOMNE

Un mois a dit : « Pourquoi L'Illustration, qui consacre chaque année aux traditionnels Salons du printemps tout un numéro, affecte-t-elle d'ignorer le jeune Salon d'automne ? [...]

PAUL CÉZANNE. — Les Baigneurs.

HENRI ROUSSEAU. — Le lion, ayant faim, se jette sur l'antilope.

CHARLES GUERIN. — Baigneuse.

J.-E. VUILLARD. — Panneau décoratif.

ALCIDE LE BEAU. — Le long du lac (Bois de Boulogne).

Article entitled
"Le Salon d'automne"
in *L'Illustration*,
Nov. 4, 1905

The Hungry Lion, enormous in its format of more than 2 × 3 meters. Its French title — *Le Lion ayant faim* — was extended into a comprehensive description of the picture: "The lion, being hungry, pounces on the antelope and devours it. Carnivorous birds have each torn a piece of flesh from the poor animal, which lets a tear escape. Sunset!" It may be that Rousseau's predatory beast in the *cage aux fauves* played some part in the name "les Fauves," which soon became a stylistic concept.

With this powerful work Rousseau triumphed at the Salon d'Automne. He could no longer be overlooked. It is true that the yearly presentation of his paintings in the Salon des Indépendants meant that everyone had finally become used to his work, and his presence at artistic events had gradually increased despite all the malice directed at him. Now, however, he was seen in association with a new generation of young artists who were making a strong showing, although their work was met with just as much disapproval as his. This new attention was expressed in particular at the end of 1905 in a double-page edition of the journal *L'Illustration*, in which Rousseau's huge painting was reproduced alongside those by Cézanne, Matisse, Derain, Vuillard, Rouault, and others, and thus, if one excludes Cézanne, within the context of the new, tumultuous movement of the Fauves. Ambroise Vollard, the well-known art dealer who handled the works of painters from Cézanne to the young Picasso, bought the painting and thereafter became Rousseau's principal dealer.

Most of Rousseau's jungle paintings were organized following the compositional model of *The Hungry Lion*: in the center foreground was the combat scene, usually shown smaller than in *The Hungry Lion*, with the forest backdrop behind, and, frequently, the complete orb of the sun or the moon up above. If it were the moon, it was always shown in its full form, never as a crescent shape. The 'protagonists' vary from painting to painting. Thus, a tiger pounces on a buffalo or attacks a scout. A panther tears at a white horse which, strangely, has wandered into the jungle. A black man is attacked by a lion. A lion kills a panther. A gorilla seizes an Indian. There are also all kinds of wildlife, mainly apes, which cavort peacefully on the forest floor or in the trees. Occasionally the jungle is just the background for a flat expanse of water where there are friendly flamingos, herons, and other waterbirds. The "cast" of the fight scenes — which all take place more or less soundlessly, so to speak — is interchangeable. Although it is true that the principal figures are always set in the center of the painting and thus give it its title, it is not here, where it is a matter of life and death, that the painting is alive, but rather primarily in the vegetation, in the rich greens

and gleaming colors, and in the jungle undergrowth and the wildlife that it conceals within it.

Rousseau used all manner of models for many of these scenes, among them a gorgeous publication about the Jardin des Plantes dating from 1845, and a no less magnificent album from the Galeries Lafayette department store entitled *Bêtes sauvages*, with the subtitle *Environ deux cents illustrations amusantes de la vie des animaux*. He seems to have been ashamed to have had this album that he plundered so often, as after his death it was found hidden away in a secret place. He thus borrowed from many sources, but what he produced in the end had nothing much in common with any one source: the result was always pure Rousseau.

For the jungle vegetation, too, he used these sources, but in contrast to the animal scenes the models here are barely perceptible; they appear to be completely integrated into the painting. He executed his forests with incredible empathy and power of imagination: the succulent, sensuous plants and grasses, the trees and the dense foliage in the deep layers, the impenetrability and yet transparency of the forest, whereby he was not troubled by worries about perspective. Usually the green of the forest is contrasted with intensely colorful, often overproportioned blooms and fruits. Now and then the petals of a gigantic white flower fall in a gigantic cascade, as, for example,

The Repast of the Lion
ca. 1907
Oil on canvas,
44 ⅞ × 63 in.
(113.7 × 160 cm)
New York,
The Metropolitan
Museum of Art;
Bequest of Sam
A. Lewisohn, 1951

Left:
Detail from
The Repast of the Lion

*Forest Landscape with
Setting Sun,*
1910
Oil on canvas
44 x 66 in.
(112 × 168 cm)
Basel, Öffentliche
Kunstsammlung,
Kunstmuseum Basel

The Snake Charmer
1907, Oil on canvas, 66 ½ × 74 ⅜ in. (169 × 189 cm)
Paris, Musée d'Orsay, on loan from the Musée
National d'Art Moderne

in *The Repast of the Lion*, where the plants, flowers, and bunches of bananas tower higher than a tree over the lion and its prey. The situation is similar in *Forest Landscape with Setting Sun* (illus. pp. 36–37), where the scene of combat becomes almost incidental beside the towering trees. The same disproportionate scale is also seen in *The Flamingos* (illus. p. 40), a depiction of a lake on the edge of a palm grove, where long-stemmed red and yellow lotus flowers stand taller than the flamingos in the foreground, although they are further away from the water, their great blooms more voluminous than the bodies of the birds on the near bank. All this has little to do with nature. These are visual decisions which in no way spring from the unconscious but from a sound artistic instinct.

Rousseau departed from the basic scheme of his jungle motif in two grandiose paintings: *The Snake Charmer* (illus. p. 38), in the Musée d'Orsay in Paris, and *The Dream* (illus. pp. 56–57), in the Museum of Modern Art in New York. Contrary to his usual custom, he dated both paintings: one 1907, the other 1910. They are both unusually large, *The Dream* being almost three meters wide — his largest work after *The Hungry Lion*.

Rousseau frequented the drawing room of the mother of his young friend Robert Delaunay, and she, at her son's suggestion, commissioned a large painting from him. Whether or not it is true that Madame Delaunay inspired Rousseau with tales of a journey to India, he chose the theme of a female snake charmer in a tropical setting. The imposing painting, almost 1.7 meters high and 1.9 meters wide, is laid out asymmetrically, which is a highly unusual composition for Rousseau. More than half the picture surface on the right is filled with the green of plants and trees, while on the left the viewer's gaze falls freely on a placid lake and the jungle on the opposite bank. The full moon is high in the sky above, its bright light illuminating the waves and outlining the dark figure of the snake charmer. She stands in silhouette, facing the front, under the foliage which extends from the right, a flute in her mouth and a snake slung around her neck. There are more snakes around her on the ground and in the branches, and a waterbird with pink plumage stands nearby. The total lack of motion that characterizes all of Rousseau's jungle paintings — except for the very first — is here provided with some explanation, through the flute music to which all of nature seems to be listening. The scene brings to mind the mythical musician Orpheus, by whom the creatures of the forest were captivated. At the same time, it sets itself within the tradition of the "noble savage," which played an important role in European, or at least French, intellectual history, at first in the figure of the "good Indian" and then, in the eighteenth century — the age of Jean-Jacques Rousseau and the great seafarers — in the paradigmatic figure of the "good Tahitian," which persisted in its effect right up to the time of Gauguin, Rousseau's contemporary. One can assume that Rousseau — who, after all, had received a certain amount of schooling — had all this in mind when he created this paradisical painting.

39

The Flamingos
ca. 1907
Oil on canvas
44 ⁷⁄₈ × 64 ¹⁄₄ in.
(114 × 163 cm)
Private collection

Eve
after 1904
Oil on canvas
24 x 18 in.
(61 x 46 cm)
Hamburg, Hamburg Kunsthalle

Combat of a Tiger and Buffalo
(first version)
1908
Oil on canvas
68 x 75 ½ in.
(172 × 191.5 cm)
Ohio, Cleveland Museum of Art

Horse Attacked by a Jaguar
1910
Oil on canvas
35 × 45 ⅝ in.
(89 × 116 cm)
Moscow, Pushkin
State Museum of
Fine Arts

Cascade
1910
Oil on canvas
45 ½ × 59 in.
(115.9 × 149.9 cm)
Collection of the Art
Institute of Chicago

Tropical Landscape: An American Indian Struggling with an Ape
1910
Oil on canvas
44 ¹¹⁄₁₆ x 63 ¹⁵⁄₁₆ in.
(114 × 162 cm)
Richmond, Virginia Museum of Fine Arts, Mellon Collection

*Tropical Forest with
Monkeys*
1910
Oil on canvas
51 x 64 in.
(130 × 162 cm)
Washington, D.C.,
National Gallery of Art

The Macaque
Photograph from the
album *Bêtes sauvages*
Paris, Galeries Lafayette

Right:
The Merry Jesters
1906
Oil on canvas
57 ³⁄₈ x 44 ⁵⁄₈ in.
(146 × 114 cm)
Philadelphia Museum
of Art

Apes Playing
1884
Illustration from
*Cent récits d'histoire
naturelle*

Right:
Exotic Landscape
1910
Oil on canvas
51 x 63 ⅔ in.
(130 × 162 cm)
Pasadena, Ca.,
The Norton Simon
Foundation

Apes in the Orange Grove
1910
Oil on canvas
45 x 63 $\frac{4}{5}$ in.
(114 x 162 cm)
New York, Ms. Adelaide Milton de Groot
Collection

Exotic Landscape
1909
Oil on canvas
55 x 51 in.
(140.6 × 129.5 cm)
Washington, D.C.,
National Gallery of Art

The Dream
1910
Oil on canvas,
80 $\frac{1}{2}$ × 117 $\frac{1}{2}$ in.
(204.5 × 298.5 cm)
New York, The
Museum of Modern
Art; Gift of Nelson
A. Rockefeller, 1954

The Dream

The Dream was the last work that Rousseau showed at the Salon des Indépendants, a few months before his death in 1910. Amid a forest landscape, again paradisical, and hardly meriting the term "jungle," a naked white woman with her hair in long braids reclines on a sofa. Together with a lion, a lioness, two birds, two monkeys, and an elephant, she is listening to the music of a black flute player who, in the dark forest, is distinguishable practically only through his flute, his brightly colored garment, and the brilliant whites of his eyes. All around are colorful flowers and fruits in lavish splendor; the jungle here is more richly decorated than in any other of Rousseau's paintings on this theme. In answer to a critic's astonished question as to how it was that a piece of domestic furniture had made its way into the jungle, Rousseau explained: "The woman, who has fallen asleep on the couch, is dreaming that she has been transported to this forest and is listening to the sounds of the flute player." The following poem was attached to the picture frame during the exhibition:

> *Yadwigha, sleeping peacefully,*
> *In a beautiful dream*
> *Hears the sounds of a shepherd's pipe*
> *Played by a friendly magician.*
> *While the moonlight is reflected*
> *On the flowers and the verdant trees,*
> *The red snakes lend their ear*
> *To the instrument's cheerful melodies.*

It is not known who Yadwigha was. There has been much conjecture about the name, which sounds Polish. Among other things it has been suggested that this might be a reference to a Polish sweetheart of the artist's youth. It might, however, also be that he was inspired by a postcard, then in circulation, which depicted a nude woman by the name of Yadwigha. Whatever the actual facts of the matter, the mysterious name does fit the painting, which has often been called — in no way authentically, although it does have a good ring to it — *Yadwigha's Dream*, or sometimes *Yadurgha's Dream*.

This is a mysterious story. But is this really, as so many people maintain, the most mysterious of Rousseau's paintings? If any of his works falls within the danger zone of the decorative, then surely it is this one, where all the plants are simply beautiful, in fact exquisitely beautiful. Surely the large painting which, more than any other, is filled with a great sense of mystery is *The Snake Charmer*, regardless of whether this lies in the music, which casts its spell over everything, the moonlight, or the painter's ingenuity.

If one wishes, one can grant the reclining Yadwigha a place among the glorious series of recumbent female nudes in the history of European painting, from Giorgione, Titian, and Tintoretto by way of Goya and Ingres to Manet's *Olympia*. But what would be gained by doing this? It produces

no insights of any kind, not even if one makes reference — as has been done — to a nude by Vallotton, who in fact takes up a similar pose on her couch. Vallotton's work was painted in 1905, five years before Rousseau's *Dream*, and was hung in the Salon d'Automne near his *Hungry Lion*, about which Vallotton published his enthusiastic article. If Rousseau was thinking of Vallotton's picture when he painted his *Dream*, this is only of interest to the extent that his own nude is completely different, right down to her pose. The comparison might possibly have some validity in its capacity to measure the "naivety" of Rousseau's depiction, but any other comparison would be equally valid. It is unnecessary to flog art history to death if nothing can come of it.

Shortly before the opening of the Salon des Indépendants, Rousseau wrote to his patron Apollinaire: "I have submitted my large picture, everybody finds it good, I think. You will unfold your literary talent and avenge me for all the insults and abuse I have experienced." In a longer text which Apollinaire afterwards published in *Intransigeant*, he wrote: "The picture radiates beauty, that is indisputable. I believe nobody will laugh this year.... Ask the painters. They are all agreed: they admire it."

Félix Vallotton
La blanche et la noire
1913
Private collection

Edouard Manet
Olympia
1862–63
Oil on canvas
51 ³⁄₈ × 74 ⁷⁄₈ in.
(130.5 × 190 cm)
Paris, Musée d'Orsay

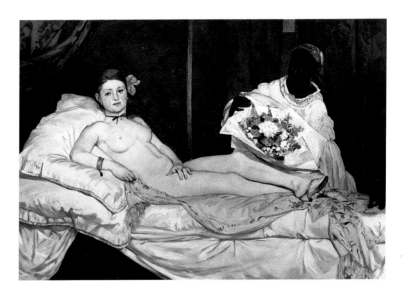

Other Themes, Other Pictures

During the years when Rousseau was painting his jungle scenes he continued to produce innumerable views of Paris, its suburbs, and the region without any noticeable stylistic changes. Rousseau, who after all was now creating large and, for that reason alone, unmissable paintings, was not too proud to turn from time to time to his familiar milieu — his small world of houses with empty windows, streets with bends in impossible perspective, street lanterns and telegraph poles, passers-by and fishermen, and the occasional airplane and airship. The motifs were repeated, but every single painting was different, and not just for topographical reasons. Again and again we find among these paintings such masterpieces as *View of Malakoff* (illus. p. 83) and *Notre-Dame: View of the Ile Saint-Louis from the Quai Henri IV* (illus. p. 61). Rousseau still avoided "big-city" Paris, even when sometimes, as in *View of the Ile Saint-Louis*, a row of multi-story houses is visible behind the landing stage on the Seine with the cathedral of Notre-Dame in the distance. He is totally at home and at ease with his subject. As soon as he leaves it all behind and enters the fantasy world of his jungles, it is as though he turns into another painter, another person.

The Bridge at Sèvres
1908
Oil on canvas
31 ½ × 47 ¼ in.
(80 × 120 cm)
Moscow, Pushkin State
Museum of Fine Arts

It would, therefore, be a mistake to regard Rousseau as an artist who specialized in jungle paintings. This was just one, rather late facet of his oeuvre, although it is true that it was the one at which he excelled. Many of his other paintings possess the specific charm of the naive, especially group pictures such as *The Wedding* (illus. p. 76), with a bridal couple, their relatives and an excessively large black dachshund in the foreground arranged in the same way as photographers were accustomed to do for group photos. Or *Old Junier's Cart* (illus. p. 75), depicting a family, in their Sunday best, on a cart drawn by a dapple-gray, and everybody, including the dog in their midst, strictly facing front, while the large black dog under the cart keeps a keen eye on a small black one running ahead. The photograph that Rousseau used as his source has been preserved. Or *The Football Players* (illus. p. 73), showing a group of men, in their striped jerseys and colored socks, surely actually playing handball or rugby with stiff, ungainly movements.

Notre Dame: View of the Ile Saint-Louis from the Quai Henri IV
1909
Oil on canvas
13 × 16 ⅛ in.
(33 × 41 cm)
Washington, D.C.,
The Phillips Collection

In addition, there were the richly figural paintings on allegorical and topical themes. For instance, *Liberty Inviting Artists to Take Part in the*

Twenty-second Exhibition of the Société des Artistes Indépendants (illus. p. 64), with the artists carrying their pictures and grouped to left and right of the lion on the Place Denfert-Rochereau in Paris, while in the sky overhead the winged figure of Liberty blows her trumpet. Or *The Representatives of Foreign Powers Arriving to Hail the Republic as a Sign of Peace*, a totally naive painting bought by Picasso, in which all the people are shown clustered together, obediently looking straight ahead, each identifiable and yet stereotyped. Or even earlier, in 1892, *A Centenary of Independence* (illus. p. 63), a painting of the Carmagnole dance whose full title is *A Century of Independence. People dance for the two Republics, that of 1792 and that of 1848, giving each other their hands to the strains of "Auprès de ma blonde, qu'il fait bon, fait bon dormir."* They dance in rings under countless banners with the Tree of Liberty in the center — a scene full of verve for which the painter received inspiration from an illustration in a contemporary magazine. And finally, from those same years, *Artillery Men* (illus. p. 74), where the soldiers are grouped around their cannon arranged in strictly frontal fashion, again with stereotyped faces, and with not a single moustache omitted — a pose probably modeled directly on a contemporary photograph.

*The Representatives of
Foreign Powers Arriving
to Hail the Republic as a
Sign of Peace*
1907
Oil on canvas
51 ¼ × 63 ⅜ in.
(130 × 161 cm)
Paris, Musée du Louvre;
Dotation Picasso

Among the portraits of Rousseau's late years, one that stands out is that of the Hungarian-born art dealer Joseph Brummer, whom Rousseau painted full-length seated in his chair. More importantly, however, he created two versions of the double portrait of Guillaume Apollinaire and his mistress, the painter Marie Laurencin, which he entitled *The Muse Inspiring the Poet* (illus. pp. 65 and 87). In addition, during these years — and we should remember that Rousseau painted for a total of not much more than twenty-five years — he produced small-format portraits, including some of children, as well as still-lifes and landscapes.

A Centenary of Independence
1892
Oil on canvas
44 ⅛ × 61 ⅞ in.
(112 × 157 cm)
Los Angeles, Ca.,
The J. Paul Getty
Museum

There is a considerable discrepancy between the jungle paintings and the others that form the vast majority of Rousseau's oeuvre. In the "other" paintings — that is, including street scenes as well as portraits and figural scenes — the *peintre naïf* cannot be overlooked, whereas in the jungle paintings he recedes to the extent that figures recede. With his jungle visions Rousseau grew beyond himself, and his petit bourgeois life, even if he only experienced the magic of the jungle in the Jardin des Plantes in Paris and in illustrations in sundry publications. It was not the case that his dreams of the jungle drove him from his milieu. He did not abandon the themes of his immediate surroundings when the distant world of the tropics called him. It was not, as with Gauguin, a flight from civilization that enticed him away to exotic forests. He still occasionally painted objects such as flying machines and hot-air balloons over the roofs of Paris, and now and then he even welcomed a factory chimney. In all of this there was nothing of Jean-Jacques Rousseau's idea of "back to nature," no longing to get back to basics, to the beginnings, about which he had even less cause to dream since he himself lived, so to speak, in basic conditions and therefore was closer to "the innocence of humanity" than those who so loved to invoke their weariness with civilization. All the people whom he painted at the

Liberty Inviting Artists to Take Part in the Twenty-second Exhibition of the Société des Artistes Indépendants
1906
Oil on canvas
68 ⅞ × 46 ⅜ in.
(175 × 118 cm)
Tokyo, National Museum of Modern Art

*The Muse Inspiring
the Poet*
1909
(second version)
Oil on canvas
57 ½ × 38 ⅕ in.
(146 × 97 cm)
Basel, Öffentliche
Kunstsammlung,
Kunstmuseum Basel

same time as his jungle scenes were still the people of his *quartier*, even
when they were the potentates of that world. In his jungle paintings he developed a stature seldom revealed in his other works. Only with them did he
place himself among the great painters of the *fin de siècle*.

Rousseau and Contemporary Artists, Poets, and Intellectuals

In his last few years young artists, poets, and men of letters entered Rousseau's life, a progressive intellectual elite who rapidly recognized the stature of this painter treading his lonely path. It was never he who initiated meetings, but always the others who sought the misunderstood painter's acquaintance as a result of the fascination emanating from his works. The first from this intellectual sphere was Alfred Jarry, who had met Rousseau much earlier and had so admired his great painting *War* that he had asked him for a lithograph based on it for his journal *L'Ymagier*.

In 1906, more than a decade later, the poet Guillaume Apollinaire asked Jarry to introduce him to the painter, whom he had become aware of through — as one could say — his "nose" for things new. In the few remaining years of Rousseau's life, and after his death, Apollinaire became his most important and most effective commentator besides the Paris-based German connoisseur and art critic Wilhelm Uhde.

In 1907 the Italian painter Ardengo Soffici, a member of the Futurists' circle, found Rousseau's *candeur poetique* appealing and bought some of his smaller works.

Another of Rousseau's late admirers was the young American painter Max Weber, who had first met him in Robert Delaunay's mother's drawing room. He too bought several small-format works, and soon afterwards — shortly after Rousseau's death — took them back with him to the United States. He showed these at an exhibition in New York at Alfred Stieglitz's 291 gallery, which played an important role in the reception of modern art in America.

Robert Delaunay
The City of Paris
1910–12
Oil on canvas
105 ⅛ × 159 ⅞ in.
(267 × 406 cm)
Paris, Musée National d'Art Moderne, Centre Georges Pompidou

The friendship with Robert Delaunay proved to be of particular significance. He revered Rousseau more than almost anyone else. It was thanks to him that Rousseau received his first major commission resulting in *The Snake Charmer*, which was shown at the Salon d'Automne in 1907, the last time that Rousseau took part in this Salon, whose president no longer desired his presence. Over the course of time Delaunay bought around twenty small-format works from his friend. In his own large painting, *The City of Paris* of 1910–12, he includes as a sort of pictorial quote and therefore an obvious tribute to Rousseau — the latter's iron bridge from the large self-portrait of 1890 (illus. p. 9). When Rousseau died in 1910, Delaunay was one of the few who accompanied the coffin. But to what extent did Rousseau, for his part, understand Delaunay's painting? He would hardly have gotten much from it. Shortly before his death he asked somebody helplessly in the course of conversation: "But why did Robert break up the Eiffel Tower?" This was a reference to one of Delaunay's pictures in which the artist makes the tower rise into the sky "step by step," in a sort of syncopation. Rousseau was unable to grasp the breaking down of all continuity, a central artistic practice for the young generation — that very same generation that was the first to recognize Rousseau's greatness. Two years after his death, Delaunay, the sculptor Constantin, Brancusi, and Rousseau's landlord, the metal caster Armand Queval, managed to put together the money necessary to obtain a three-year lease on a suitable spot for Rousseau's remains in the cemetery of

Bagneux, near Paris. Brancusi and Ortiz de Zarate chiseled a short poem by Apollinaire on the tombstone in 1913.

Rousseau's friendship with Wilhelm Uhde also dated from 1907. Uhde was then married to Sonia Terk, later the wife of Delaunay. It was Delaunay who arranged the first meeting between Uhde and Rousseau. Uhde bought paintings from Rousseau as well. In 1911 he published the first monograph on Rousseau, a not very extensive one, but certainly affectionate. And a year later he organized the artist's first major exhibition at the Galerie Bernheim-Jeune.

In November 1908 Rousseau invited everybody to a large soirée in his studio. As always on such occasions, his acquaintances from the *quartier* and his music and art pupils also took part, mingling with Apollinaire and Marie Laurencin and the painters Francis Picabia and Maurice Utrillo. In that year Picasso held an improvised banquet in his studio in the legendary Bateau-Lavoir in Montmartre that has gone down in history as "Le Banquet Rousseau." Among the participants were, besides Picasso, his mistress at that time, Fernande Olivier, Apollinaire, Laurencin, Georges Braque, the poet Max Jacob, the art critics Andre Salmon and Maurice Raynal, and the American writer Gertrude Stein and her brother Leo. All of them later gave reports of the bizarre evening, each account more or less differing from the others. "Le Banquet Rousseau" was a mixture of artistic affair and homage to the much older painter, whom they looked up to but whom they also mocked in a friendly way. The climax of the evening came when Apollinaire recited a long poem about the guest of honor. What has survived above all else are the words that Rousseau directed at his host Picasso in his speech of thanks: "We two are the greatest painters of our time, you in the Egyptian style and I in the modern style."

Henri Rousseau died on September 2, 1910, aged sixty-six. As, according to his own account, he had only begun to paint when he was forty, his creative period spanned less than a quarter-century. His fame grew rapidly after his death. Already in the following year works by him, arranged by Wassily Kandinsky, featured in the memorable "Blauer Reiter" exhibition in Munich: seven paintings owned by Wilhelm Uhde, which were also reproduced in the "Almanac" of the same name. In his contribution "Uber die Formfrage" Kandinsky wrote: "Henri Rousseau opened the way for the new possibilities of simplicity." In 1913 the "First German Autumn Salon" in Berlin had an entire room filled with works by Rousseau. In 1914 Apollinaire dedicated Number 20 of his *Soirées de Paris* to the *Douanier*. Monographs on Rousseau by Adolphe Basler, André Salmon, Philippe Soupault, and Christian Zervos appeared in 1927. In 1936 *The Snake Charmer* was hung in the Louvre, and on the occasion of the 1937 exhibition "Maîtres populaires de la réalité," the Association des Amis d'Henri Rousseau was founded. The Musée d'Art Moderne de la Ville de Paris celebrated the painter's centenary at the end of 1944 with an important exhibition. Rousseau had finally found his place among France's great painters.

Symbolism

Even if Rousseau's jungle paintings only represent a small part of his artistic output, they are nevertheless that part on which his fame is primarily based. They are the most complete and perfect of what he produced in the last six or seven years of his life, with the exception of *Surprise!*, painted in 1891. Many of his other paintings possess great magic, but one would not use the word "perfection" in connection with them. Their charm can certainly also be attributed to their awkwardness; they breathe the world of the "little people." The jungle paintings, however, go far beyond this. They too, like the paintings of streets and squares, have their basis in reality, but it is the reality of the botanical garden, heightened and taken into the realms of fantasy. Here — and only here — Rousseau had visions. Here he fulfilled his great dream, which also had a childlike component in that it was a dream that children dream. In his day — the age of the "industrial revolution" and of rapidly growing cities — palm trees and other exotic plants were part of the decoration of elegant homes and inner courtyards, as compensation for the sobriety of real life — one could say as a flight into an imagined reality. Accordingly, one could see Rousseau's jungles as typical of their time if they were not painted in such an objective way, so lacking in a sense of reverie that contemporaries eager for the Orient and the exotic were unable to recognize their dreams in them. Neither Rousseau's jungles nor Gauguin's Polynesian paradises corresponded to what was paraded as exotic in the drawing rooms of the well-off and in the great exhibitions of the day. Such yearnings were far better satisfied by Salon painting with *its* exoticism, *its* Orient, and *its* palm trees.

One is tempted to associate Rousseau with the Symbolist movement of the turn of the century. But nor did Symbolists recognize him as one of their own, neither Gauguin nor Odilon Redon, who both knew him personally, let alone such painters as Gustave Moreau and all the others. In fact there is nothing of the Symbolist in Rousseau. His absolute representational objectivity, which dominates even in his otherwise fantastic jungle paintings, prevents any classification with the Symbolism of his time. In particular his colors are never charged with a "higher" meaning, but are always "merely" the colors of things, even when they are invented colors allocated to things for compositional and decorative reasons; they never have symbolic value. Despite all his freedom of invention and all his visual imagination, everything remains objective and material. The sensuousness of his painting excludes the supernatural. Only very rarely — in *The Sleeping Gypsy* and in *The Snake Charmer* — is a mystery evoked that goes beyond the bare facts of the situation. These are exceptions in Rousseau's oeuvre, although they are probably his most beautiful and expressive paintings.

The Decorative

Nonetheless, Rousseau's jungle paintings did correspond to the times in which they were created, but for a quite different reason: they were, and are, decorative in the highest degree. The term "decorative" has become a pejorative one as a consequence of the ornamental excesses of Art Nouveau, which led to a strict purist counter-reaction in all sectors of the visual arts. But this was not the case in Rousseau's day, in other words at the time of Art Nouveau, in which such great artists as Gauguin, van Gogh, and Munch were involved. The decorative lay on the line of a declared return to the principles of surface and large-scale composition, through which the opposition to the Impressionists' dissolution of form was primarily expressed. Having been frowned upon by the Impressionists, surface and composition were again given their due. There was a trend towards mural painting, to *grand décor*, the intention being to create a link to the wall-painting tradition of the great early civilizations of Egypt, Rome, and the early Renaissance. Not only among actual classicists such as Puvis de Chavannes, but also in Gauguin's circle, was there talk of classicism, traditionalism, synthetism, and the renewal of decorative art.

Rousseau fitted into this overall picture of painting in the late nineteenth century. Although on the one hand he stood outside history, on the other he did belong to the generation of Post-Impressionists who took as their cause all that the Impressionists had spurned: surface, form, and composition, the clarity of things. Even Georges Seurat, who forced the Impressionists' disintegration of form furthest with his pointillist technique, arrived in this manner at a new stabilization of figure and object, and of the painting as such. The often-quoted statement by the Symbolist painter Maurice Denis dating from 1890 also applies to Rousseau's works: "Remember that a picture, before it is a warhorse, a female nude, or some anecdote, is essentially a flat surface covered with colors assembled in a certain order." Or at least this statement applies to Rousseau to the extent that it applies to the painters for whom it was coined. His jungle paintings are "flat surfaces covered with colors." But they are also images of the jungle that are more than just color and form, in the same way that Denis' own pictures are not just "flat surfaces" but, as Symbolist works, express meanings, often of a religious type, which reduce the force of Denis' maxim. Rousseau's closeness to the highly decorative manifestations of another contemporary movement, Art Nouveau — for instance, the extravagant floral book designs of someone such as William Morris — is obvious. The pictorial tapestries of the late Middle Ages, too, of which people felt reminded so frequently in Rousseau's day, were extremely decorative arenas for fantastic happenings.

This was all particularly well expressed by Delaunay, ten years after his friend's death, in the essay "Henri Rousseau le Douanier" in the magazine *L'Amour de l'Art*:

"Rousseau takes shape alongside the masters who herald modern art and sometimes outdoes them with his strong conviction, his naivety, and his sense of style.... Rousseau's style strives for perfection. But he had no theories.... Without ever talking about style and tradition, Rousseau was more impregnated with them than most painters of his generation. The picture was for him a primary surface with which he reckoned physically in order to project his thoughts on it. But his thinking consisted solely of visual elements. If order and composition formed the basis, the content was distributed according to the structure of the picture. The picture was a whole. Everything was subordinated to the inter-relationship of the surfaces on the primary surface of the canvas."

Paul Gauguin
Excellent Days (Nave nave mahama)
1896
Oil on canvas
37 × 40 ½ in.
(94 × 103 cm)
Lyon, Musée des Beaux Arts

There is no doubt that, if Rousseau's jungle paintings had been "merely" decorative, they would hardly have been able to arouse the admiration of the Surrealists. For these artists Rousseau's works had completely different, contrasting qualities, thanks to which they recognized in his paintings forerunners of what they themselves were producing. It was the unconscious or the preconscious that they saw at work in Rousseau, and naturally also the fantastic, the dreamlike, the mysterious: distance from reality even when — or perhaps especially when — it was combined with a maximum closeness to reality. This gulf between extreme objectivity and exotic fantasy lifts Rousseau's jungle paintings above any suspicion of being "merely" decorative, which does not however prevent them from having a highly decorative quality in their luxuriant vegetation, their colorful flowers, blossoms, and fruits set in green surroundings, and their perfectly round suns and moons above tropical scenery. Whether or not one wishes to call this decorative, Rousseau had an extraordinary natural genius for color.

He also had an inner compass that pointed towards harmony. Despite the murderous and yet so harmless scenes that take place in the jungle paintings, they radiate a great sense of harmony. Perhaps it was this that Rousseau meant by "completeness": that the many individual elements should combine together harmoniously to form a great, tranquil whole. The way in which he distributes objects and colors on sometimes very large picture surfaces is instinctively "right." Even in such a radically asymmetrical picture as *The Snake Charmer*, everything is balanced, and here again we find the complete equilibrium of a classical painting. A strong rhythmic feeling is inherent in Rousseau's work. All of his paintings are steeped in rhythm, both in color and in form. Rousseau "composed" his paintings with a mastery that is all the more astonishing since there was nothing masterful in his own modest life. And this is not just true of his large paintings, but equally so of each of his townscapes; everywhere there is harmony and balance. This goal of achieving "completeness" must have been more important to him than anything else.

The "Naive" Painter

Was Rousseau a naive painter? It is right to class him among *peintres naïfs*? Can a great artist ever really be naive?

One does not need to define the term "naive" to answer this in the affirmative. Rousseau was naive in his poetry and in his composing and music-making. He was naive in the relatively few comments that we know of that he made about life, for example the famous speech he gave during "Le Banquet Rousseau" in Picasso's studio. He was naive in his letters, for instance the one to the mayor of Laval or in others to a woman named Leonie whom he was courting until a few months before his death. In any case, he was naive by comparison with the other great artists of his time and the way in which they lived: they all moved on a totally different intellectual level, especially in their discussions about questions of art. Fernand Léger, who knew Rousseau well, once wrote in an article about him: "He did not recognize the qualities of his works, he had a confused, but sure awareness of them." In the same article, he recalls a joint visit to an exhibition of the works of Jacques-Louis David where Rousseau particularly admired the execution of the hands, something that he himself could never achieve. At the time, he said to Léger: "I must learn to draw." Léger adds: "That was his mistake. Fortunately he never had the time to take drawing lessons."

The Football Players, 1908
Oil on canvas
39 ½ × 31 ⅝ in.
(100.5 × 80.3 cm)
New York, The Solomon
R. Guggenheim Museum

Artillery Men
ca. 1893–95
Oil on canvas
31 ⅛ × 39 in.
(79.1 × 98.9 cm)
New York,
The Solomon
R. Guggenheim
Museum

In any event we feel Rousseau's figural representations to be naive. These most clearly reveal his clumsiness, particularly striking and touching in the allegorical and topical paintings which have an apotheotic exuberance. Nor can one call *The Football Players* of 1908 anything but naive (illus. p. 73). The same is true of *The Wedding* (illus. p. 76), *Old Junier's Cart* (illus. p. 75), and even the two versions of *The Muse Inspiring the Poet*, the double portrait of Apollinaire and Marie Laurencin (illus. pp. 65 and 87). There can be no denying Rousseau's naivety as soon as he begins to deal with figures. This is true even of the many minor figures — such as passers-by and fishermen — in his city views: a mostly toylike, tiny world, occasionally with flying machines depicted in the sky in a childlike manner. The viewer finds himself loving the aspect of the childlike, the naive, and the *anima candida* in these paintings before becoming aware of the magic of their form and color, quite unlike the jungle paintings where — although the figures are also seen in a childlike manner — this hardly matters due to the profusion of tropical vegetation.

A final sign of the childlike is the additive principle of Rousseau's painting, which also applies to the jungle scenes. What Rousseau depicts is in the original sense an enumeration, just as we see in paintings done by children. At the same time, however, everything fits into the compositional arrangement of his works, most ingeniously in the jungle paintings, which are seen large even when they are made up of innumerable details. In these Rousseau gives hardly any impression of being a naive painter, least of all in *The Snake Charmer*, a masterpiece in which the question of the naive does not even arise.

An occasional attempt is made to deny Rousseau's naivety in view of his stature. This is understandable, since all over the world there are "Sunday painters" among whom one would hesitate to class him. In fact, Wilhelm Uhde played a part in this by setting him alongside such "naive" painters as Camille Bombois, Louis Vivin, André Beauchant, and Séraphine Louis, even if he did rate Rousseau much more highly. Many authors even believe that Rousseau deliberately stylized himself as naive. Supporting this view is the fact that his sketches were executed in a much freer, much less naive, and much more mature manner. Given their artistic freedom, the step to the simple and clumsy in his paintings appears to be a deliberate step back into the childlike that he actually did not need to make.

This is supported by the remarkable statement made by Rousseau to a critic shortly before he died, that the painters Gérôme and Clément had always advised him to retain his naivety. This could, in fact, give rise to the impression that he was deliberately playing the role of the naive person that everyone thought him to be. However, the fact that he was aware of his naivety does not mean that he was not naive. It was also a naive trait to admire the work of professional academic painters and suffer because he was not able to

Old Junier's Cart
1908
Oil on canvas
38 ¼ × 50 ⅞ in.
(97 × 129 cm)
Paris, Musée de l'Orangerie;
Jean Walter – Paul Guillaume Collection

The Wedding
1904–05
Oil on canvas
64 ¼ × 44 ⅞ in.
(163 × 114 cm)
Paris, Musée de
l'Orangerie;
Jean Walter – Paul
Guillaume Collection

match them. Great painters may have self-doubts — that is almost a general rule. But a painter of Rousseau's stature who in no way recognizes his own greatness and who admires and envies eclectic virtuosi must be called naive. This does not, however, alter his greatness. While conversing with André Malraux, Picasso once remarked of Rousseau: "Father Rousseau was not a better naive painter than others, but a colorist of genius who was naive."

Rousseau and the Young Artists

Rousseau's "discovery" by young artists shortly after the turn of the century coincided with those same artists' "discovery" of the art of Black Africa and Oceania. "Primitive" art fascinated them and so, therefore, did original and, as they thought, instinctive art. Unnaturalistic, pre-naturalistic artistic expressions were more highly rated than was the art of classical antiquity and the Renaissance, which had dominated the horizon for so long. Naturalistic talent was discredited. The unskillful, the clumsy, and the awkward were held to be of higher value. An African wooden statue was preferred to a marble sculpture by Praxiteles. Even drawings by children were acknowledged as valuable artistic expressions. All this meant a step of spectacular proportions. A completely new artistic world picture emerged, prepared for by movements in late nineteenth-century art such as Impressionism and Neo-Impressionism, but now with a totally new radicality.

Thus it was that a phenomenon such as Rousseau could step into the foreground as a matter of course after having for so long been laughed at and derided. "Mockery about simplemindedness is transformed into admiration of simplicity," Friedrich Schiller said in 1795 in his famous essay, "Naive und sentimentalische Dichtung," written a century before Rousseau painted.

The young artists were enthusiastic about Rousseau. But did he also influence them? Did he leave any traces in their art? Did the admiration they felt for him all of a sudden have any effect on their own art?

Such influences have been sought and, here and there, are thought to have been found. For instance, it was said that the mandolin in a Braque still-life of 1901 is reminiscent of that in Rousseau's *The Sleeping Gypsy*. But these are little more than peripheral similarities. They do not take us into the center of the painter's art. Braque and Picasso — in other words, the Cubists — were impressed by the *Douanier*, but there was no need for this to have had any effect on their art. Why should it? We tend to place too much emphasis on such influences. It is a mistake to conclude that artistic fascination must inevitably lead to a direct influence on another artist's oeuvre. Thus, in general, the influence of African art, which so enthralled Picasso, Braque, and so many others, is often overestimated.

The crucial thing was that perceptions had changed and thus it was almost inevitable that the art of Black Africa would become the focus of artists after even Gauguin, who, after all, spent part of his life on Tahiti and the Marquesas, but was blind to the art of Oceania. A sort of watershed separated the generations of Gauguin and Picasso. Gauguin's horizon was formed by the early high civilizations of Egypt, India, and Indonesia. Even the statues that appear in many of his paintings have more similarity with the art of India than with "primitive" art. After Gauguin, Africa stepped into the foreground. As for influences, there are hardly any. Picasso's *période nègre* was, as was known for a long time, not actually a "negro period" at all, even if African masks clearly did play some part in his principal work at that time, *Les Demoiselles d'Avignon*. It did not go much beyond that. It is striking that it is precisely those who were the first to "discover" African art in the Musée du Trocadero in Paris and in simple bric-a-brac shops — namely, the Fauves — Matisse, Derain, Vlaminck — who do not show the slightest influence of it

Portrait of a Woman
ca. 1895
Oil on canvas
63 x 41 ⁵⁄₁₆ in.
(160 × 105 cm)
Paris, Musée du
Louvre; Dotation
Picasso

in their work (although it is also true that there were almost no opportunities for them to do this since their art was limited to landscapes and still-lifes). It was the smaller minds among the artists whose paintings and sculptures reveal direct influences.

Pablo Picasso
Portrait of Maya
1938
Oil on canvas
28 ⁴/₅ × 23 ²/₃ in.
(73 × 60 cm)
Paris, Musée Picasso

Child with Doll
ca. 1904–05
Oil on canvas
26 ³/₈ × 20 ¹/₂ in.
(67 × 52 cm)
Paris, Musée de
l'Orangerie;
Jean Walter – Paul
Guillaume Collection

In 1907, the year that he created *Les Demoiselles d'Avignon*, Picasso bought a full-length portrait of a woman by Rousseau from a dealer for five francs. No connection of any kind is known. However, it may seem surprising that this painting was so pleasing to Picasso at this critical juncture in his artistic development. Much later, at the end of the 1930s, his portraits of children are directly reminiscent of Rousseau's paintings of small children. The relationship is so striking that it seems unlikely that Picasso was not conscious of it. Probably it was the associative closeness of the theme of "child" to that of the "childlikeness" of Rousseau for which these echoes are to be thanked. Around this time, Rousseau was not an important figure for Picasso; the moment of his relevance in Picasso's consciousness was long since past. Rousseau was simply a painter to whom Picasso still felt drawn, so to speak, a familiar and admired colleague and *copain* down through the decades.

It is no surprise that the Surrealists, since the 1920s, had taken pleasure in Rousseau's jungle paintings. They automatically laid claim to him as someone who had his place in the genealogy of "fantastic art" over the course of art history, as a predecessor of their own thoughts and creations. André

Joan Miró
*Vegetable Garden
with Donkey*
1918
Oil on canvas
25 ¼ × 27 ½ in.
(64 × 70 cm)
Stockholm, Moderna
Museet

Breton, their spokesman, often mentions Rousseau in his writings. But only rarely is a direct influence found, even in Surrealism. Rousseau's presence is sensed in many of Joan Miró's early works, particularly *Vegetable Garden with Donkey* of 1918, in the pronounced naivety and the delight in the smallest details. Yet these paintings are still pre-Surrealist. Much later, Miró wrote that he was influenced by van Gogh, Rousseau, and Picasso in the years between 1916 and 1920. However, some of Max Ernst's forest scenes of the 1930s are truly and unmistakably "Rousseauesque" (illus. p. 81). In fact, it is difficult not to think of Rousseau when observing them, especially as here — as in Rousseau's jungles — the visionary fantasy goes hand in hand with an extreme, almost botanical objectivity in the depiction of the plants, although these are in no way exotic. But this was only a phase in Ernst's art, and moreover again falls outside the time when Rousseau's actual hour in the art of the twentieth century struck.

Should we include the painters of the Neue Sachlichkeit movement in Germany? Of course they knew and admired Rousseau, but in their romantic and idyllic mood rather than in their social-critical and aggressive

aspects. Here again, however, no significant influences are to be noted. As the simple, the childlike, and the innocent were favored, it was obvious to invoke the *Douanier*, who in the meantime was also well-known in Germany. But in this case it was the jungle paintings that made the least impression, because the German painters were concerned with the domestic, the near at hand, not with exotic far-off lands. The jungle remained Rousseau's own domain.

Naive painting flourished in this climate. This "genre" was not, however, particularly relevant in the art of the twentieth century. Rousseau's friend and biographer, Wilhelm Uhde, had opened up the way with his life-long endeavors. Over the decades untold numbers of *peintres naïfs* could have invoked the name of Rousseau, if his towering stature had not been such that people were hardly prepared to classify him as a practitioner of *peinture naïf*. Thanks to his place in art history, Rousseau was so far above everything else that was produced — charming though it may have been — that it is pointless to explore the influences that can be detected here and there.

Rousseau and Léger

Rousseau had a significant effect on just one of the great painters of the first half of the twentieth century — Fernand Léger. In his case, this influence was expressed not just in peripheral, coincidental aspects. One does not immediately think of Rousseau when viewing Léger's work; on the contrary, Léger was a totally different spirit and in truth in no way "naive." Nevertheless there were many links with Rousseau. He made his acquaintance with him in 1907 through Delaunay, and he paid him frequent visits. In this so very different painter he recognized a related visual intention and related principles, although for Rousseau — unlike Léger — these did not have the character of principles: for him, they were natural, unreflected artistic practices, based not on any ideology. Much of what Léger advocated with great passion — clarity, simplicity, and objectivity of forms, colors, and things — he found had already been put into effect by Rousseau, forty years his senior. He admired the great harmony in Rousseau's oeuvre, and, of course, the decorative and the leaning towards the monumental, but also — and this was particularly important for him — the absence of any "sentimental"

Fernand Léger
The Three Musicians
1930
Oil on canvas
46 ³⁄₈ × 44 ³⁄₄ in.
(118 × 113.5 cm)
Wuppertal, Von der
Heydt-Museum

View of Malakoff
1908
Oil on canvas
18 1/8 × 21 5/8 in. (46 × 55 cm)
Private collection

Fernand Léger
Level Crossing
1912
Oil on canvas
36 5/8 × 31 7/8 in. (93 × 81 cm)
Basel, Ernst Beyeler Collection

values. Léger saw himself as standing in a great classical tradition, in contrast to another basic historical current that he called "romantic," and he sometimes said that the "classical" current extended from the "primitive masters" — by which, in accordance with French usage, he meant the painters of the fifteenth century — via Poussin, David, Ingres, and Corot, down to Rousseau. On another occasion, he said of Rousseau: "Classical, static art and the French line of Fouquet, Clouet, Le Nain, David, Ingres: those were the artists he revered."

Fernand Léger
Mother and Child
1922
Oil on canvas
36 $\frac{1}{4}$ × 25 $\frac{3}{8}$ in.
(92 × 64.5 cm)
Basel, Öffentliche
Kunstsammlung,
Kunstmuseum Basel

Fernand Léger
The Readers
1924
Oil on canvas
44 $\frac{7}{8}$ × 57 $\frac{1}{2}$ in.
(114 × 146 cm)
Paris, Musée Nationale
d'Art Moderne, Centre
Georges Pompidou

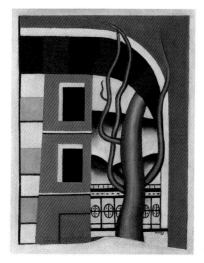

Fernand Léger
The Tree
1925
Oil on canvas
25 ½ × 19 ¾ in.
(65 × 50 cm)
Hanover, Sprengel
Museum

Banks of the Bièvre,
Spring
ca. 1904
Oil on canvas
21 ½ × 18 in.
(54.5 × 45 cm)
New York,
The Metropolitan
Museum of Art

Léger's own yearning for folk art — an art that was close to ordinary people — was fulfilled in the work of Rousseau. Although he rarely referred to it directly in his many speeches and writings, Léger loved this painter who could do nothing else but speak a language that for him, Léger, was program and postulate. If he frequently praised the "argot," the slang of the common people — their specific manner of expressing themselves, which he maintained corresponded to the artistic idiom of modern artists — this showed the closeness of the two painters: this is illustrated most clearly in *The Three Musicians* of 1930 (illus. p. 82). He once wrote:

"Poetic sensitivity is innate in the common people. Who except the man in the street creates and renews the spoken poetry of argot day after day? With their inexhaustible power of creation ordinary people transform the reality of their everyday life. And what do modern artists do? Exactly the same thing! Our pictures are our argot. In them we transform objects, forms and colors. Should it then be so difficult to understand them and get closer to them?"

In fact, Léger was wrong in his conclusion: his art was not able to bring him closer to the common people to whom he felt such attachment. Nor could his love for Rousseau's art be reciprocated. He wrote of a visit with

Rousseau to the Salon des Indépendants: "The new art, which to him was totally incomprehensible, has not influenced him at all....Believe me, in his deepest heart he was thinking: the only lovely picture here is my own."

Léger enjoyed the signals of progress included by Rousseau with the greatest matter-of-factness as an intrusion into his idyllic landscapes and city views: the telegraph poles, iron bridges, flying machines, and not least the Eiffel Tower. "Don't forget," wrote Léger, "that the master of us all, Douanier Rousseau, fifty years ago dared to include telegraph poles, with their pretty parallel insulators in his landscapes." The best illustration of this is a comparison of Léger's *Level Crossing* of 1912 and Rousseau's *View of Malakoff* (both illus. p. 83). Both Rousseau and Léger were highly prosaic poets.

A much more obvious and tangible effect of Rousseau's work on Léger's came after the early contacts, a decade after the *Douanier's* death, and even then it was not in the form of marginal echoes but significant in that it concerned agreement in the essentials. How, for example, could the succulent plant in Léger's great painting *Mother and Child* of 1922 (illus. p. 84), which reappears in many of his other works, have been created without reference to Rousseau's jungle vegetation? Or the flowers that women hold

Fernand Léger
The Three Figures
1924
Oil on canvas
51 × 51 in.
(129.5 × 129.5 cm)
Private collection

The Muse Inspiring the Poet
1908–09
(first version)
Oil on canvas
51 ½ × 38 ⅛ in.
(131 × 97 cm)
Moscow, The Pushkin
State Museum of
Fine Arts

in their hands in many of Léger's paintings of the early 1920s — for instance *The Readers* of 1924 (illus. p. 84): are they not reminiscent of the long-stemmed, leafless blooms seen in many of Rousseau's landscapes? They are different, certainly, but comparable in their austerity, their clarity, and their abstraction. Or denuded branches — for example, in Léger's *The Tree* of 1925 (illus. p. 85) — which remind us of the snake-like plant elements in paintings of Rousseau's. These are all much more than coincidences; they are indications of a deep visual relationship.

A striking example of the closeness between the two great painters is seen in Léger's *The Three Figures* of 1924 (illus. p. 86), where the man on the right directly evokes the figure of Apollinaire in Rousseau's double portrait in the position of his head and in the way his hand grips the scroll. In Léger's case, this too is, of course, a conscious treatment of reality: conscious as regards form and style — ideologically conscious. Obviously, a one-sided dialogue with Rousseau is taking place here. Léger formalizes what in Rousseau is natural, even clumsy, and yet masterly. This becomes particularly clear if we compare Rousseau's *Portrait of Pierre Loti* with Léger's *The Mechanic* of 1918. Léger's latter figure is, in any case, reminiscent of Rousseau's in his closeness to the people, his simplicity, and not least his walrus moustache befitting his social status, as though Léger had taken one of Rousseau's many moustachioed characters and painted him in profile. Each figure holds a cigarette in his right hand, and the pose is the same, but what in Rousseau's hand — which stands out so starkly against the subject's dark suit — appears unskilled and gauche, is in Léger's hand — where the cigarette is held apparently just as awkwardly held between the fingers — a bold composition dictated by the artist's creative will.

Finally, one has to think of Léger in connection with the frontal, rather ceremonial, stereotyped anonymity of Rousseau's faces — frequently attributed to his photographic models —this obvious expression of genuine naivety in the one artist and deliberate naivety in the other. With these paintings of the "Sunday picture" type, Léger had a vision of a blissfully happy

Portrait of Pierre Loti
ca. 1891
Oil on canvas
24 × 19 ¾ in.
(61 × 50 cm)
Zurich, Kunsthaus
Zurich

Fernand Léger
The Mechanic
1918
Oil on canvas
25 ⅝ × 21 ¼ in.
(65 × 54 cm)
Villeneuve d'Ascq,
Musée d'Art Moderne

human community, filled with general equality and fraternity among human beings. It was his modern way of dreaming of that "innocence of humanity" that Rousseau's human representations possess quite naturally.

In 1948–49 Léger painted *Homage to Louis David*. The title is written on a piece of paper that the girl reclining in the foreground holds in her hand. It was his homage to the great master of the French Revolution. Equally well, and perhaps with even deeper artistic justification, the painting could be entitled *Homage to Henri Rousseau*.

Fernand Léger
Homage to Louis David
(*Leisure Time*)
1948–49
Oil on canvas
60 ⅝ × 72 ⅞ in.
(154 × 185 cm)
Paris, Musée National
d'Art Moderne, Centre
Georges Pompidou

Chronology

1844	Henri-Julien-Félix Rousseau is born in Laval on May 21.
1861	Family moves to Angers.
1863	Released from military service, and enters the employment of a lawyer in Angers
	As a result of minor theft, he is sentenced to one month in prison. To avoid this, he enlists for seven years' military service in Angers.
1868	Death of his father.
1869	Marriage to Clémence Boitard in Paris.
	Napoléon III declares war on Prussia. Rousseau is in Dreux as a regimental reservist.
1872	Employed by the *Octroi*, the Parisian customs service.
1885	Awarded a diploma by the Académie Littéraire et Musicale de France for his composition "Clémence, waltz with introduction for violin and mandolin."
	Receives a copyist's permit from the Ministry of Culture, giving him free entry to the major museums.
1886	First participation in the Salon des Indépendants, where he shows four paintings, including *A Carnival Evening*.
	Participation thereafter every year except 1899 and 1900.
1888	Death of his wife Clémence.
1889	World Exposition in Paris.
	Writes a vaudeville in three acts, *Une Visite à l'Exposition de 1889*.
1890	*Myself, Portrait-Landscape* exhibited at the Salon des Indépendants.
	Death of his mother.

1891	First jungle painting, *Surprise!*, exhibited at the Salon des Indépendants.
1893	Leaves the Parisian customs service.
	War shown at the Salon des Indépendants.
	Makes the acquaintance of Alfred Jarry.
1897	*The Sleeping Gypsy* shown at the Salon des Indépendants.
1898	Vain attempt to sell *The Sleeping Gypsy* to the town of Laval.

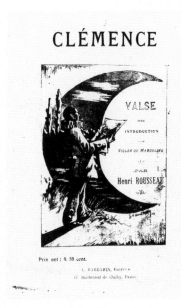

1899	Writes a play, *La Vengeance d'une orpheline russe*.
	Marriage to Joséphine Noury.
After 1900	Gives music and painting lessons in his own home.
1901–04	Gives lessons at the Association Philotechnique in painting on faience and porcelain, watercolors, and drawing.
1903	Death of his second wife, Joséphine.
1905	First participation at the Salon d'Automne, including *The Hungry Lion*.
	The Hungry Lion is reproduced in *L'Illustration* alongside reproductions of paintings by Cézanne and the Fauves.
	Vain attempt to sell *The Hungry Lion* to the French state.
1906	Makes the acquaintance of Guillaume Apollinaire.
	Ambroise Vollard buys *The Hungry Lion*.
1907	Start of friendships with Robert Delaunay, Wilhelm Uhde, and Max Weber.
	For the last time takes part in the Salon d'Automne, including *The Snake Charmer*.
	Sentenced to prison because of a fraud case in which he was involved.

After 1908 Holds "soirées musicales et familiales" at his home.
     "Le Banquet Rousseau" is held in Picasso's studio.

1910   *The Dream* exhibited at the Salon des Indépendants
     Rousseau dies on September 2.

Sources of Illustrations

Page 21: © 1997 The Barnes Foundation™, all rights reserved
Pages 24–25: Photographie Giraudon
Pages 34–35: © 1984 The Metropolitan Museum of Art
Pages 36–37: Martin Bühler
Page 41: Co Elke Walford, Hamburg
Page 48–49: Virginia Museum of Fine Arts
Page 51: The Philadelphia Museum of Art
Pages 50, 55: National Gallery of Art, Washington, D.C.

All other picture material is from the Prestel archives.

Selected Bibliography

Adolf Basler, *Henri Rousseau*, Paris, 1927
Lise and Otto Bihalij-Merin, *Henri Rousseau*, Dresden, 1971
Henri Certigny, *La Vérité sur le Douanier Rousseau*, Paris, 1961
Douglas Cooper, *Rousseau*, Paris, 1951
Pierre Courthion, *Henri Rousseau*, Paris, 1956
Pierre Descuarges, *Le Douanier Rousseau*, Geneva, 1972
Frank Elgar, *Rousseau*, Paris, 1980
Yann le Pichon, *le Monde du Douanier Rousseau*, Paris, 1981
André Salmon, *Henri Rousseau dit le Douanier*, Paris, 1927
André Salmon, *Henri Rousseau*, Paris, 1962
Philippe Soupault, *Henri Rousseau le Douanier*, Paris, 1927
Cornelia Stabenow, *Henri Rousseau: Die Dschungelbilder*, Munich, 1984
Wilhelm Uhde, *Henri Rousseau*, Paris, 1911
Dora Vallier, *Henri Rousseau*, Cologne, 1961
Christian Zervos, *Rousseau*, Paris, 1927

Most Significant Exhibition Catalogue:

Le Douanier Rousseau, catalogue to the exhibition in the Grand Palais, Paris, and in The Museum of Modern Art, New York, 1984–85. With essays by Roger Shattuck, Henri Béhar, Michel Hoog, Carolyn Lanchner, and William Rubin.

Pegasus *Library*

Beckmann and the Self by Sister Wendy Beckett

Cézanne in Provence by Evmarie Schmitt

Marc Chagall: Daphnis and Chloe

Dalí: Genius, Obsession, and Lust by Ralf Schiebler

Edgar Degas: Dancers and Nudes by Lillian Schacherl

Paul Gauguin: Images from the South Seas by Eckhard Hollmann

Van Gogh in Arles by Alfred Nemeczek

Edward Hopper: Portraits of America by Wieland Schmied

Wassily Kandinsky and Gabriele Münter by Annegret Hoberg

Gustav Klimt: Painter of Women by Susanna Partsch

Kokoschka and Alma Mahler by Alfred Weidinger

Edouard Manet: Images of Parisian Life by Hajo Düchting

Miró in Mallorca by Barbara Catoir

Amedeo Modilgliani: Portraits and Nudes by Anette Kruszynski

Monet at Giverny by Karin Sagner-Düchting

Picasso's World of Children by Werner Spies

Renoir: Paris and the Belle Epoque by Karin Sagner-Düchting

Auguste Rodin and Camille Claudel by J.A. Schmoll gen. Eisenwerth

Egon Schiele: Eros and Passion by Klaus Albrecht Schröder

Titian: Nymph and Shepherd by John Berger and Katya Berger Andreadakis

Toulouse-Lautrec: The Soul of Monmartre by Reinhold Heller

Très Riches Heures: Behind the Gothic Masterpiece by Lillian Schacherl

Turner on Tour by Inge Herold

Paul Klee: Painting Music by Hajo Düchting

Prestel
Munich · New York